THE KATHLEEN PARTRIDGE SERIES

Kathleen Partridge's Book of Faith
Kathleen Partridge's Book of Flowers
Kathleen Partridge's Book of Friendship
Kathleen Partridge's Book of Golden Thoughts
Kathleen Partridge's Book of Happiness
Kathleen Partridge's Book of Hope
Kathleen Partridge's Book of Seasons
Kathleen Partridge's Book of Tranquil Moments

Illustrations by Jane Watkins

Edited by Donald Greig

Designed and produced by Visual Image, Craigend, Brimley Hill,
Churchstanton, Taunton, Somerset TA3 7QH

First published in Great Britain in 1997 by
Jarrold Publishing Ltd, Whitefriars, Norwich NR3 1TR
Reprinted in 1999

ISBN 0-7117-0902-5

Printed by Proost, Belgium 2/99

Kathleen Partridge's
BOOK OF
Friendship

Kathleen Partridge

Friendship

Old friends are like old shoes
They are so fitted to the years,
They know our highest efforts
And discern our secret fears.

They've walked with us and waited
When we aimed for better things,
Through embarrassment or glory
Poor as paupers, proud as kings.

And though for various reasons
Shoes wear out and friendships end,
We lose part of our lives
Each time we quarrel with a friend.

To Lift the Heart

Think of a lovely landscape
If ever you droop with despair,
Picture the perfumed pathways
The dells and the arbours there.

Sit in a shady corner
Or lounge on a sunny slope,
Where nature brings you contentment
And God will offer you hope.

Borrowed Joy

Let's borrow from our memories
When times are sad and trying,
Let's find a little laughter
When we're very near to crying.

Secure in loving thought
Of happy friends and distant places,
Knowing future days will hold
Good times and merry faces.

Far Reaching

We never know how far our influence reaches,
How much our daily deeds and manners count,
Our outlook and our actions are reflected,
If only by a very small amount.

By being mean, we can make others petty,
By being just, we can make others fair,
If quarrelsome, we draw folks into quarrels,
If generous, we make the others share.

And that's the only way the world grows better,
Gradually overcoming greed;
The finest way to wipe out vast dissension –
By every individual's thought and deed.

High Hopes

May your hopes run clear
As the waters of life
And high as the shining blue,
And all the love
That you gave to life
Come back on the tide to you.

May the colour of dreams
That dry your tears
Be gold as the morning glow,
Bringing a blessing
Along the years
To the dearest people you know.

Bless You

God be with you in the morning
In the sunshine or the rain,
In the magic of each moment
As the day begins again.

God be with you in the evening
When the day has reached its goal,
When all creatures cuddle closely
And the lamb bleats near the foal.

Though life's duties are demanding
And your path is not sublime,
Through the ups and downs of living
God be with you, friend of mine.

Friend of Mine

Fear not dear friend, sleep well, be brave
In peace of mind your strength to save,
Lean on the one who understands
Trust in the skill of healing hands.

Then every hour of every day
Will help you farther on your way
To health and vigour, free from dread,
To live the happy life ahead.

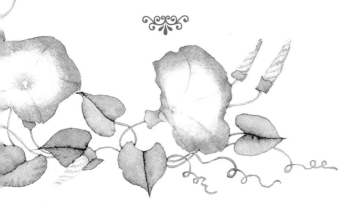

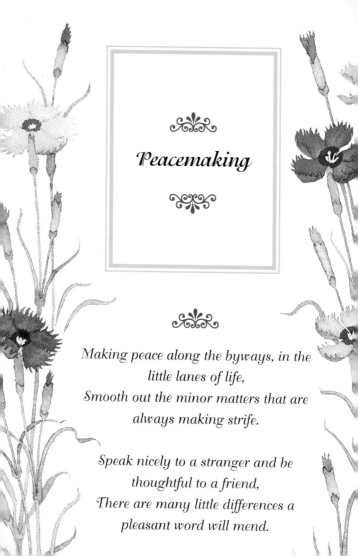

Peacemaking

Making peace along the byways, in the little lanes of life,
Smooth out the minor matters that are always making strife.

Speak nicely to a stranger and be thoughtful to a friend,
There are many little differences a pleasant word will mend.

In every homely circle there is someone
who must be . . .
A peacemaker, a diplomat to help the
rest agree.

And even if we cannot spread our
wings and travel far,
There's such a lot of quiet work to do
just where we are.

So many dismal moods to cheer and
sunbeams to release,
The world has room for many more
disciples of the peace.

Your Home

Never be shy of inviting folks back
Because of the luxuries that you may lack,
Better be frank than be known as a fraud
And be proud of the home that your purse can afford.

A friend worth the knowing will like you the more
For the good-hearted welcome that waits at your door,
For the honesty that you display in your voice
When you live there and like it, because you've no choice.

Generosity

Nice to be generous with your car and lift
folk here and there,
To fill an empty back seat on an outing
anywhere;
But better still to choose the ones without
cars of their own,
Who might have spent a sunny Sunday
afternoon alone.

It's pleasant to be friendly with the people
near at hand,
To include an extra one in little parties that
are planned;
But better still to choose the one who hasn't
much to do,
Who is rather poor and cannot offer
outings back to you.

*You're tempted to invite the bright
successes much admired,
Who have a crowd of dates, whose
company is much desired;
But how much greater to include the lesser
known and shy,
To make a point of sharing pleasure with
the smaller fry.*

Faithful Heart

Faithful, what a lovely word for anyone to earn;
Through all the turmoil of the world to feel you can
return
To just one faithful heart that is not shaken by
events,
That stays as true through adverse circumstances
and comments.

Faithfulness is one great virtue that can never pall,
That keeps its value all the time while fortunes rise
and fall,
Companions come and go, and good times visit and
depart,
Thank God if you can count among your friends,
one faithful heart.

The Link Still Holds

The space between our letters seems to lengthen,
The evening finds us over-tired to write,
And so we drift away without intention
From those whose friendship brought us such
delight.
Yet in our thoughts the memory is golden,
The happiness once shared again unfolds,
And all the lovely wishes for their welfare
Rise from a heart to prove the link still holds.

Be Happy Friend

The flowers that springtime promised
Have bloomed in winter's wake,
Old troubles grow less wearisome
And hearts forget to ache.

Maybe love lies bleeding
But the flax will never fail,
And orchids are a miracle
That make the sun turn pale.

The scilla bells are ringing
With the sweetest music yet,
Calling all who listen
To forgive and to forget.

Popularity

It isn't those who yearn for popularity who gain it,
Nor yet the ones who go about pretending to
disdain it,
But those who simply carry on whatever day may
bring,
And find the smallest reason to be cheerful and to
sing;
Who have no time for envy, and who make light
work of cares,
But treasure and enjoy the happy moments that
are theirs.
Such people gather friends, for they are friendly
without trying,
They kindle confidences where they wouldn't
dream of prying,
Other folk are pleased to meet them, friends are
happy when they call –
Not expecting popularity, they're popular with all.

All Friends Together

An old fashioned garden of old fashioned flowers,
Tansy and teasle on bankside and bowers,
A friendly profusion of lily and phlox
Carnations and cornflowers, verbena and stocks.

The pathways are peaceful, the moss is caressing,
The scent of the lavender offers a blessing,
And somewhere a sundial is telling the hours
In a friendly old garden of old fashioned flowers.

Broken Hearted

I bid you love remember
When you are fancy free
That not so very long ago
You were attached to me.

Chrysanthemums you sent me
Gold as the sun above
Knowing that the meaning of these flowers
Was 'slighted love'.

So press this petal in a book
And on some distant day
You'll open it to take a look
And steal my heart away.

The Coming of Friends

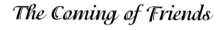

We long for you and look for you
In wintry winds and rain,
Waiting for your visit
To make us young again.

Forsythia, grape hyacinths
And hawthorn down the dell,
All of them will blossom
In time to wish you well.

Catkins in the copses
And violets in the hollow,
Carpeting the footpaths
For friendly feet to follow.